Train to the City

by Alicia Alvarez
illustrated by Jeremy Tugeau

Joan had grown up in this log cabin.
Now her family was planning to live
in the big city.

Dad was driving the wagon to
the coast.
She and Mom were taking the red
and white train.
The train was the quickest way to go.

3

Joan cried as she got on the train.

She tried to be happy.

But she would miss Dad's jokes.

She would miss her hens' chicks.

At first the train was slow.

It crossed a low bridge over a little
stream.

Then it went faster and faster.

It raced past the bright lights of cities.
It streaked by rows and rows
of wheat.
Then it stopped with a screech.

"It is huge," said Joan.

"How will Dad find us in such a big place?

"We've got a plan," said Mom.

"We'll meet him on Main Street."

Every day, they waited for Dad.

At last, a line of wagons came.

"It's Dad!" cried Joan.

Joan and Mom ran to give Dad
a hug.

Target Phonics Skills

Endings -er, -est
faster
quickest
-dge/j/
bridge
Long a: ai, ay
day
Main
train
waited
way
Long e: ea
stream
wheat
Long i: ie, igh
bright
cried
lights
tried

Long o: ow, oa
coast
grown
Joan
low
rows
slow
Possessives
Dad's
hens'
Endings
cities
cried
crossed
driving
raced
stopped
taking
tried

Consonant Blends
screech
streaked
stream
street
Syllables
cabin
family
happy
little
planning
wagon
wagons
Unit 5 High-Frequency Words
find
live
over
would

Word Count 166

MY SiDEWALKS ON
SCOTT FORESMAN
READING STREET

UNIT 5

PEARSON
Scott Foresman

scottforesman.com

ISBN 0-328-21401-9

90000

9 780328 214013

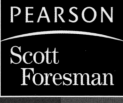

Level A5